Son

A Collection of Poetry Unchained

Kristin E. Hiett

Publisher: Let Her Glow Publishing House
Printed in The United States.
ISBN: 979-8-9945614-0-9

SILHOUETTE

Native: Sonoma County, California

As in any creative endeavor, diverse mediums frequently provide the driving force necessary to push one's self to the next creative level.

If creative guidelines were to limit us to one style, one medium or one arrangement, the craft of visual expression and rhetoric would be only words and pictures of little meaning all telling the same story. The breadth of any creation falls to completion for an artist, when through the eyes of each beholder, the meaning portrays an individual interpretation.

Art is but poetry and poetry a song where the music meets all mediums in between.

As so, my poetry evolves from a visual of the weaving of words from poetry to song, to paper and pen, to canvas with color, and back again. I see those as inseparable.

I am grateful to the creator, who many times sends a whisper from his angels to speak through my work, or, in some cases, through the inspiration of an old soul. Beauty is embellished through many mediums. The art of seeing it formed from majestic simplicity, by whatever means, is left to the beholder's imagination...

-*Kristin*

CONTENTS

CHAPTER 1
MIRROR OF MYSELF

Somewhere in Time

Follow me everyday, to a place where I have been,
it's the means to experience, but never to an end.

Lost in an instant, I follow Father time,
though windows of the now,
and the conscience of my mind...Somewhere in Time

I see the world through different eyes
a land in which I can't describe,
I'm caught half way between,
a fantasy and a dream.

Searching for the answers
reaching for beliefs,
wishing I could understand,
the anomalies I see.

Like a child who is learning,
and always wanting more,
I have a pocket full of logic
in my mind's eye stored.

I'm collecting it all the time,
tucked away for raining days,
to revisit in good time,
perfectly designed and sits in my confines.

To anyone who seeks,
there is a promise you will find,
it's written in the universe,
and etched in the purest light.

Outside of me I'm looking,
there is no measurement of time,
I'm not anywhere but everywhere,
I'm somewhere, in time....

A Mile Away

I'm a mile away from finding the home where I grew up.
So much has changed around it, I hardly know what's what.
It doesn't look the same, my familiar old hometown—
the road is old and weary, and fences falling down.

I walked this way a thousand times,
down this old dirt road,
kicking cans, singing kid songs,
the mountains weren't so old.

Riding bikes and catching butterflies,
swinging from eucalyptus trees at night.
Picking berries by the abandoned well,
sliding in boxes down the grassy hills.
Throwing stones and pebbles in the wind—
I thought it would never end.

Picking pears right off the trees,
it never was a sin.
Bouncing balls and creepy crawls,
collecting all of them.

The sun shined while it rained,
right through the window panes.
Dreams were real-life chapters
that got me through the days.

Now cobwebs and the spiders
call my home their own.
Shutters all but falling,
and the paint is cracked and worn.

I'd give so much to spend one day
back in those old times,
when life was so simplistic
and but a gentle rhyme.

Caution

Moving forward with caution,
I tiptoe down this crossing.

Careful, say the signs,
proceed at *your* own risk,
but temptation swept me under,
within its clouded midst.

Dread that creeps into my bones,
beguiles my stately will,
each time I take this step,
I purge to no avail and fall into a silence
for a lesson to be still.

It is wonderful for the most,
sublime to say the least,
that is, until it's time for me,
to taste the bitter sweet.

My burden seems to bring you bliss,
which preys upon my weakness,
my tears that fall can't penetrate
the mortar of your fortress.

This vessel falls so weary,
the outlook of a future,
portrays it all so eerie.

Have I played this act before?
For certain, I would remember,
and spread a word of caution,
to those who may come after.

A Pointed Vision

A pointed vision faced the old man,
tortured by epic dreams of a pre-existence.

A cogent notion slipped through his aging hands.

Aimlessly, he prods his way down moth-eaten memories
that feast unmercifully on his unsuspecting grief—until
he questions the logic of his own validity.

Caught within a blackened void of space,
he lies pathetically inert.
Questions run rapid through his frail estate,
seven times seven.

Reliving all that he has wagered,
before his eyes it crumbles;
again,
in ruin,
again,
reduced into a molecule of waste.

His body trembles; he sees an old man toil relentlessly
as the circle of history falls complete.

The vision transcends—a re-run of
another time, another place...
He weeps silently, but the
tears fall too late, as they faintly whisper
his allotted fate.

A Queen Who Has No Name

There's a garden in the forest that is sheltered by the trees,
and a waterfall majestic, that collects the fallen leaves.

Shadows cast in darkness, a hush over the scene,
that dims the brilliant colors, of the eucalyptus trees.

I've lost my way, getting far from myself –
I can't find the path from which I came...
It seems I'm winning or I'm losing, at my own symbolic game.

Drinking in the rain, I'm feeling quite insane,
searching though the hollows of this twisted refrain.

Through a smoke colored cloud, I've never seen before,
there appears to be a key that may open any door.
I'm reaching high to touch it but it's fading at my grasp...
it seems to my good sense, it may be no easy task.

The castle from a distance, that sits upon a hill,
is far above the forest, of the story that I tell.
The caretaker of this place, is a man who has no face,
he dwells beneath the dungeon,
where his fate sustains in waste.

The castle you may not enter...for you surely shall not leave,
tis hard to understand, or even to believe...
but those who've enter willingly, vanished from their dream
and left behind the remnants of a notion pre-conceived.

There are four Kings in the courtyard,
and a Queen who has no name...
she's calling for assistance, she looks to be in pain...

The Queen calls to her court, come solve these mysteries,
the King is standing idle by as her army then retreats.
The highest priest is called, to give a salutation,
but he disappeared before he spoke, much to her trepidation.

I close my eyes to ponder all, in my bated haste,
contemplating my escape, I see no time to waste.
So is this real, I ask myself with question so precise,
or just a figment conjured up by my over active mind?

Alas…

This fairy tale of which I tell, could be a paradox indeed,
and I wonder will I wake up and remember what I've seen?

By Your Hand

By your hand a miracle flows –
from your finger tips…
Caressing strokes from lines unknown,
the vision you depict.

Idle Wither

That which held it beauty,
thru years of weathered time,
now cast unto the graveyard,
of waste and lost design.

Once shiny new, then slightly used,
now sits in idle wither,
worth nothing less than salvage,
That can't go back together.

The Last Two Days

The last two decades I have sustained.
The last two years I've not lived in vein.
The last two months have afforded me pain.
The last two days have left their remains.
The last two hours brought reflection, but little gain.
The last two seconds were exactly the same.

A Little Tale

When death separates a love,
and time steals away what once was,
turn around and you will begin to believe,
time has not been good to thee.

When a tale of time, has reached its hour,
and you bid farewell to this tangible flower,
will you wonder before you lie life down,
how did you spend this time around?

Logic, Sin and Consciousness

In search for straight-out answers
that come from where within,
I closed my eyes and searched the realm
of logic, sin, and consciousness.

As I hurled over peaks,
crossing beyond the miles
that turned to many weeks,
I found a hole that didn't stop—
it appeared to be an empty spot.

Colors raced so bright they hurt;
I kept on going to get there first.
Ice cubes floating over fields of grass
turned into goats that melted fast.

A life-like toad with a funny hat
tipped his drink from a see-through glass.
A bold white sheep with a missing tooth
lied to me about his youth.

A talking road sign winked and laughed;
this trip was not an easy task.
I dare say I saw these things—
for one would think I'd be insane—but
roosters crowed for no reason at all;
I understood their chicken call.

Upside down a bat did fly,
his wings weren't black, but white.
He saw as well as myself, while
flying his bat-shaped kite.

This funny bear did a cartwheel in the air,
as if he hadn't the slightest care.

Still my questions remained unanswered,
until I saw my sweetheart dancing.
Now to each his own shall seek the truth,
in whatever way they choose.

It all became surreal thereafter,
as I turned the page
to the very next chapter.

Tired Bones

Lost days and dusty roads,
winding rivers that run too close.
Memories flow from an empty heart—
I find myself alone.

Purple haze running down my spine,
norther's brewing in a muddy sky.
Two ships passing side by side,
in three-foot waves and rolling tides;
it makes me fear what might have been—
I think of that now and then.

Too far gone to say goodbye,
misty water fills my eyes.
I'm too tired to ponder my life,
it's not proper for a man to cry.

As reality runs its course,
my dreams decay like a dusty corpse.

Streaks of thunder light the sky,
so loud it hurts my eyes.
Thinking about my carnal ways—
it's bound to put me in an early grave.

Looking for nothing down nowhere roads,
I'm living on the air, sleeping on stones, I'm growing old.
I can't get past these tired bones.

Render

Render the shield that hides the grace,
and toss it to the deepest grave.

Render me compliant now,
till mercy has her way.

I am only human,
which falls to no surprise,
when the truth is buried far beneath,
the closing of my eyes.

Pardon me for what I've said,
give lenience to my soul,
my Father I have come undone,
it's time to make me whole.

Poetry Unchained

What sleeping secrets lie,
in my esoteric mind,
so safe within the hollowed rim
of these clearly haunted eyes?

Poetry unchained…

There it goes again,
my imagination can't refrain,
if only I could understand,
just where it all begins.

A glimpse of what is to come,
a promise broken come undone;
second sigh, unfolds the light,
emerging into one.

Poetry unchained…

The evidence although contrite,
eludes the face of time;
my inherent nature interacts,
expressing life through rhyme.

I Planted a Seed

I planted a seed in the garden of life.
I watered it often with prayers and smiles.
It grew to be a living thing, its roots were planted deep,
it brought me joy so sweet.

At not a warning the roots died without a reason,
for there was not even a change of season.
Plucked from where it called home,
and buried cold and alone.

I seemed senseless that the seed grew and lived,
it was a alive with purpose then
an untimely death rendered worthless.
Perhaps I planted this seed in a place it was not meant to be,
I prayed through its death,
I could mourn and then try to accept.

Beautiful Rose

A porcelain rose sits still on a shelf
it has no scent nor can it melt.
It's beauty will never be conveyed,
it's but a molded, painted piece of clay.

Parallel to life and matter, there is
no direction for its seeds to scatter.
For a living rose dies too soon
It falls to the ground, and then life resumes.

The faux rose housed on it's shelf tis
true it will never wilt, but when it
falls from it's occupied space, it shatters
to pieces when it breaks.

I like the living rose,
have bloomed in life and faced my foes,
but, if I sat upon a shelf and should I fall
from where I dwelt, I would break into a thousand me's
and be buried amongst a million rose seeds.

Love on the Rocks

In the still of the night,
the waters subdued,
Earth is melodically set in tune.
Two lovers embrace in the light of the moon
that shines in the night, halfway through,
and the stars a million miles away
set a timely mood.

One kiss upon her lips
began a perfect process.

Two souls lost to love,
completely unsurpassed.
Surrendered in protective arms,
rendered unto trust;
we put aside all doubts and fears
fallen unto us.

A once-depicted fantasy
portrayed inside of me,
is now a perfect picture,
in a perfect memory.

Music is Me

Music is me, through me,
in me a sounding breeze.

Melody new, melody old,
waving through timeless portals,
a story it unfolds…

Sunshine, rain—its music refrains,
a melody soft or resounding roar,
it's all about the score.
Lyric to string, music to me is everything—
writing a wrong when love is gone,
is best said through a song.

Music is love that transcends,
a sound that never ends.

Music is free, music is me.

Pleasing Ransom

Flittering angels seem kept at bay,
as visions of halos dance round my head.
Such lovely creatures flowing on air
surround me where I lay.

My eyes appear open, but I cannot see
through the willowy shadows
of these images around me.

This feeling of what is taking place
is a reality somewhat hard to take,
for I'm a bit uneasy at this situation—
caught up in moments of reflection,
a hostage of this pleasing ransom.
I can't... I can't stop dancing.

Mother Earth

Rosemary, cloves, and Mother Earth
all dance the ancient theme,
in renaissance to angels
and all created things.

Celebrate in unison,
for all to share this day;
the knights in shining buckler
stand ready and at bay.

Revelry still prances
on ships not meant to see;
participation's shallow,
and I'm weary to my knees.

Broad is the spectrum,
and baffling as it seems—
it's time to put away the lies
and summons honesty.

Obscure Beginning

Bathed within this strange abode,
yet strangely secure within this home.

Excited as the time draws near,
I feel a pang of unknown fear.

From this haven, I question my future survival,
amidst a world outside which awaits my arrival.
I hunger for something, yet my stomach is full.

I sense a change nearing,
beyond my mortal control, and I question—
will I lose the window to my very soul?

A metamorphosis of an unfamiliar sight,
an obscure beginning in another ghostly light.

Mirror Mirror

Black spots and haze, tarnished by old age,
jealousy seethes from your withered gaze.
Reflecting an image revealing,
something quite unappealing.

In a lost dimension of glittering glare,
a hostility lies in your glassy stare.
Vanity lures your prey, then tricks them into
another day. Steel eyes, hypnotize—
another poor fool falls for your disguise.

Truculently, you continue to fade,
oh mirror of false prophecy and gaze,
how is it you change us from day to day?

Through the window of my eyes,
I watch you fall to your demise.

So shattered is your glass,
lay tiny pieces within the frame of brass.
My eye does open, and my vision fades…
as I brush my hair to prepare for my day.

Mirror, Mirror on the wall, your reflective lies aren't funny at all..

Tears of God

I want to touch a rainbow
and feel her colors flow.
I'd like to hold a moonbeam
and watch its radiant glow.

I wish to talk to angels,
entranced within their light,
to learn of where they come from,
and what their existence may be like.

To feel the newness of life again,
as a babe in the womb ascends—
almost a frightening thought,
starting all over again.

To feel the rain upon my lips
as it falls from the heavens above,
the tears of God spilling adrift
upon the mountain tops.

Before I leave this Earth,
I long to learn more of our Universe,
where someday my spirit must return,
to that which I was, before my birth.

This Tear

In sadness I surrender and bend my head to shame,
the last and final tear shall fall, but will not fall in vain.

I can't regret the meaning, nor brush aside the pain,
in restless walks I wander, to sort my options once again.

Time has come upon me as hours tick away,
the more I am attached, the greater this price to pay.

I fear for the oppression and openly confess,
my choice has come to pass—
I've taken the easy access.

I Heard Your Cries

Acid rain fell in your heart one day,
those clouds, it seems, could not fade.

You just needed a sympathetic ear,
to get you through your doubts and jumbled fears.

I heard your cries from somewhere in space,
I could not ease your pain, nor help to erase.

I conversed with you by order of meditation—
take care, my thoughts, lead not to trepidation.

I conjured pure love sent by means of the light,
and waltzed with you all the night.

When the morn, she gave her golden light,
it set you back on the road of life.

Once I Had a Lover

Once I had a lover,
we sailed across the seas,
and spoke of far off places
someday we hoped to see.

A sip of wine, a drink of tea,
we lounged upon his balcony.

As we listened well to one another,
a cross word never passed our lips;
each night we fell to each other's arms
and sealed it with a kiss.

Books we relished and discussed,
music, a melodic muse was a must.

Art was the art of its own muse,
and beauty took form from another view.
We laughed and cried and shared many pleasures;
every moment together was a perfect gesture.

Once I had a lover,
a mentor
a teacher like no other.
My best friend, my bed friend, my everything.
It seems so long ago, he left not for another,
but for to be alone.

Now on our own,
my light is dimmed,
the night turns winder cold,
the wine now sour grapes,
the leaves have turned to brown and gold.

Books without an ending, far off places I'll never see,
nor stories with no beginning, to be discussed with me.

Alas I've come to let it go,
but memories run deep,
as the winter cold upon my brow,
rain falls beneath my feet.

A Different Door

Our souls were familiar the moment we met.
Our hearts remembered our very first kiss.

Two spirits reunited, waking from a long hiatus,
hidden behind the beat of our hearts,
when destiny had torn us apart
and dropped us in another plane,
never to speak one another's name.

It was a perfect union—nothing changed,
your mannerisms remain the same.
I can live again through your eyes,
that tell me of days far gone by.
Behold the knowledge of things old,
that continue to unfold.

You cannot find your peace within
when searching for sweet release,
only empty parlors filled
with the strangers you meet.

Bitterness was a lesson of lost treasures,
a test of character and strength,
of a life that tethers.

I know you now as before—
you simply opened a different door.

Lies Of Honor (Wakan Tanka)

By the river, I sit,
remembering times when the sun earned my braids
and the dust of the Earth stuck to my skin,
becoming one with my flesh.
I feel the chill of the wind now; the seasons will change soon,
and I grow older with each moon.

I have seen horses rise in battle,
and the arrows form a blanket
of sticks and feathers through the sky.
Babies cried, and children fought a war passed down
from chiefs and elders of olden days—
to uphold the honor of their land, their tribe,
and their fathers before them.

Bodies of red and white lie lifeless, one atop the other;
souls snatched from hollow shells, left to rot in open graves.
It was to the natives that Mother willed this land,
for we nurtured her,
taking only that which provided food and cover.

We sought not to pollute nor taint her,
but to honor her.
Those who slaughtered our tribes
and watered the land with our blood
have dirtied the sacred ground
and stripped her of her dignity.

Mother Nature weeps—her tears have turned to sulfur,
her soul to the filth from trash made by those who took the fat.

Wakan Tanka, oh Great Spirit in the Sky,
forgive the massacre of your sons and daughters,
and bury their bones with honor and love.
For those who govern with hatred,
no rest shall befall their souls.

My Promise Forever

Through the portals of time, love has always been…
From the first created entities which marked the joining
of male and female, came the laws of a union that were
written in the winds of the perpetual universe.

My love begins here and now,
and will remain a constant to you forever.

This vow I take, this commitment,
I etch on the scroll of the tablets of God, before God,
I consecrate my body and soul to you in his presence.

In the years to come, whether they be paved with serenity
or troublesome times, I will stand beside you
with honor and truth,
abiding with the promise I make to you today.

I will love you forever, for always,
and though this vessel may cease to exist,
the love that emanates from the spirit shall survive
eternity and, as evolution continues,
so shall my love, though space or gender
and back to the light of God
until the circle begins again.

No Compromise

Look into his eyes to search for the truth,
the eyes will tell you what you already knew.

Tears will fall and weal up in side,
from things suspected, but clearly denied.

Mistrust consumes you, sets you up for the fall,
in the circles of promise dishonesty calls.

Tension grows stronger, steals your sweet peace,
cinders burn hotter, with no means for release.

Empty reflections state back at you,
things are said and misconstrued.

Surrounding dissension broken rules recalled,
barriers unseen from invisible walls.

No Compromise...
just unpleasant words,
no time to hear
what needs to be heard.

Last bow taken,
no turning back,
when the curtain falls,
on the final act.

Space Junk
2005

CHAPTER 2

e…l…l…i…p…s…i…s…

In the Midst

In the midst of the morning
as dawn breaks her light,
thoughts cursed me
nearly all through the night.
The hands of time ticked on and on,
from here to beyond.

As I walked through the valleys
and through the peaks,
it's become apparent—
it is time to retreat.

I saw men and angels at my side,
politely begging for my time.
I felt nothing and heard much less—
it was a particle of my penitence, I guess.

In arbitrary declarations,
lost in thoughts of my recollections,
such despair petitioned in my prayer;
I still feel quite demure,
for homage made out loud
are but empty and unclear.

Efforts I make to abandon those moments
render me a helpless component.
Finally, at break of light,
hoping for peace to fall,
I am able to turn my flight
to another port of call.

With a long, deep breath,
I loosen my soul,
and give flight
to meet the fairest of all.

Where Angels Don't Reside...

The Angels don't live here anymore,
they packed up their wings and went away,
in hope to find a better place.

This side of town was just too much,
with all its garage and disgust.

No apropos to this behavior,
no pocket religion offering a savior.

Defecation on crumbling streets,
where the dorms of self-degradation retreat.

Sold to the highest bidder in the city,
ten minutes later, no self pity.

And there it goes, another piece of my soul,
each time I fall victim to this life I chose.

Then I think of an adoring one,
with touch so kind and known to none;
a sober breath and tender words
that redeems me from sin and hurt.

Reality steals my dream, cutting through my esteem,
for in front of me is a feast of sluts and slugs,
who sacrifice their love for drugs.
Twenty bucks and a run of bad luck,
gets you nothing much.

There's the one who keeps me fried,
and the Johnny-come-latelys who could care less if I died.
No thanks to the drug king and biker queen,
they deserve no awards for birthing me.

What angel would ever stand with me?
Is my fate is written on eternity?

The Balance Between

To every storm there is a calm,
to every right there is a wrong;
to every lyric there is a song,
and life continues on.

To every promise there's a break,
to every give there is a take;
to every dream there is a theme,
to every moon, there is a beam.

To every crush there is a fling,
to every circle there is a ring;
to every body there is a soul,
to every half there is a whole.

To every heart a beat, for every wake, a sleep;
to every find there is a seek.

For every try, there's a pass by,
to every heartbreak, a cry;
to every deny there is an accept,
and for every birth, there is a death.

The balance between,
is nothing more, than fate unforeseen,
we blindly walk that lonesome road,
until our destiny unfolds.

For every sonnet there is a time,
to every poem, a rhyme.

Nothing Wagered

If you desire love to flow,
before eternity's last call,
then choose to live again,
and choose to forgive your sin.

Does love then come more than once?
It is the luck of the draw that falls to a hunch.

Sometimes we fall to it many times over
and each time we grow a bit more sober.

When feelings change and times get rough,
that special love is never enough.

If all love were the same,
nothing wagered, nothing gained.

Prophecy

The conscience is filled with jumbled thoughts,
blank is the target of a split-second shot.
Shades of darkness fall apart,
in search for an open mark.

Impractical litigation, opinions formed
in expectation—and now I see the mold
in which the Creator holds.

Wisdom from the unidentifiable
is relentlessly unreliable.
There are directions for simple minds,
who bring the balance between day and night.

Left to the substance of what is hoped for but not yet seen,
is the assurance of existence by way of omnipotent means.

Onward to the question: What is to be redeemed,
and what is necessary to believe?

I cast my unawareness beyond the shore of the desert's sea,
and place my insecurities
at the cross, on bended knees.

The Flight of His Rendition

It lies beneath the shelter,
of there purple rain,
a factor so intense,
it shakes the golden grain.

A rumble can be heard
throughout the universe,
traveling to the suns
without a spoken word.

Survival of all ages -
the telepathic mind,
like a fog it waves to us,
in symbolic signs.

Yet we scarce believe
not more than what we dream,
as evolution signals us
by mishap and non belief.

The creator of the universe
shares freely of his wisdom,
to those who wish to undertake,
the flight of his rendition.

Left with My Tears

Are you still here, my love? Or,
are you drifting into yourself again?

Do you still want me near my love? Or,
are you loosening your embrace again?

Your eyes wander aimlessly at times,
I'm lost then as to what is on your mind.

You are so visible within my sight,
but sometimes you are as far away
as a thought— as years of light.

Love scares you so,
your eyes say it's true.

Perhaps your heart still beacons another,
and you heaven't the energy to love any further.

I can have patience if my efforts are revered,
but once again,
I face the fact—
I may be left with my tears.

The Realm of Dream Stealers

Where do these trenches run
that taunts my conscience?
I am not amused.

Tatter me in a million parts
and scatter me throughout the universe,
as if doubt should be my muse.

Forward my faculties to a dimension
of passive far from the nonsense;
help me escape the realm of expectations put upon me
by well-meaning dream stealers and thieves.

Drenched in hypocrisy,
the mournful meanings of anti-wisdom wails
loud as the untruths scatter
by mouths of dragons and arm chair kings.

I'm ripped from the arms
of comfort and sanctity.
I long to be nestled in the drapes
of a long gray beard of knowledge.

This life journey becomes more perplexed,
as I watch it all implode it's mess..

Petals at My Feet

On a bed I lie with petals of roses at my feet,
abundance of red, a dozen I think.

Velvet and lovely, I feel compassion
for this delicate flower now void of action.

Once seeds that floated in the wind,
etched from the tides of time,
until they give up an earthly life.

Rue of Grace

I see a void in recent times, that wraps the world in
sentences that do not rhyme.
The masses confined,
the contempt that runs the circle of time.

I've looked it through and through,
see it in and out,
nothing precludes the question, the doubt.

Through the hesitation and fear,
the connotation of poor decision,
lurking far and near,
is not without distorted vision.

If one could step from their vessel,
the ship in which we dwell,
and could see their faux performance,
what would it reveal?

The times of least compassion,
and bitter trails of bits,
tossed to those who swallow,
but blinded by its darkness.

I observe quite quickly,
adults in wrongful deeds;
unruly children are more pleasing
then the sight of those I see.

The pathetic mass of matter
they occupies their space
is ill-learned of empathy,
mercy, love or grace.

Such rue upon their face—
those without compassion or grace.

Spirit of Beauty

You sailed into my life like a soft summer rain,
and took my soul to heights unknown;
you taught me how to love again.

Here is what I saw

Rainbows dancing across moonlit nights,
of tomorrow on a never-ending screen of life.

A spiritual awakening in another being
is a paradigm of someone changing.

Through cons of another existence not yet revealed,
I must have known you intimately, but kept it well concealed.

You rocked me with pleasures of empyrean delight,
into the wee hours of morning, and then into the night.

Here is what I know

It's an honor to have seen
the beauty of your being,
to pass the form of this earthly shell
in a quiet, sweet reveal.

Like the ocean waves breaking
as the tides roll into shore,
so quietly awaking
the loveliness of your—

eyes that spoke to me words that need not be said,
eyes that healed my fears of matters to be dread.

The walls did fall when your eyes met mine;
illusions turned riddles into lovely rhyme.
Nothing in heaven or on earth could steal from me
such sweet love, given by you so beautifully.

Relics

Where it begins,
finish to end…
Shallow waters twist and bend
to distance theatrics of rendition.

Such relics never change;
questions so do remain.
Superstitions thought insane,
beliefs of such lie in vain.

Days of miracles die to dreams
that once gave way, by way of means.

Portals of hope laid asunder,
lifeless, tucked and hidden under.
Spirit of man, soul of thy depth—
some empowered, some inept.

Ancient objects quite unknown,
speaking clearly to certain ones;
others see nothing, to none.
Answers rest in other folds,
guides whose stories often told,
shed answers right before our eyes—
blind are most, and quite unwise.

We don't believe our lying eyes, but dismiss
the rest, and let it lie.

Dance of Defiance

Dance with danger,
and it will consume you,
in depths of lost illusion.

A tangled web weaved so well,
the unsuspecting could not tell.

Weave it in, and weave it out,
to and fro, here and about,
through lost devotion—innocent emotion.

A prisoner of this dark alliance,
dances, the dance—
of its defiance.

Sweet Freedom

Strings attached to unwanted dreams,
like Irish pendants that hang from my jeans.

Those dangling strings I did so dread,
spun a web of armor from my heart to my head.

I wished you out of my mind a thousand times,
Why don't you vanish from me and live your life?

I hated seeing you again, it made me think of sweet revenge;
old wounds resurface, turning me inside out,
then, I remembered why I had my doubts.

I pondered for a moment, wishing I could hide,
I just stood there as you walked away, picking up your stride.

It was then I knew, you were free from my mind,
I had thrown you into the abyss of time.

I, finally free, once again, feel once again like me.

Ah.. sweet freedom, first bitter, then, sweet as Eden.

The Universe is Me

Searching for my passion's fire,
seems labeled as a false desire.
A dream or just a fantasy,
I really can't aspire.

My virtues are aligned,
according to my mind's eye,
and a path now set before me,
in this cycle they call time.

The Universe is calling
to the center of my now;
it's me who lingers in this world,
surrounded by my doubts.

There is a sign that points to somewhere,
transparent as it seems—
it is my badge of no regrets,
for the Universe is me.

CHASM
MOMENTS

CHAPTER 3

CHASM MOMENTS

A Strange Night's Ride

I took the strangest ride,
the day before last night…
If I hadn't been there myself,
I'd think it was a lie.

I rode a crystal light beam
on the back of a horse that couldn't be seen.
She was fast in the air for an old gray mare,
and she pranced by the midnight rain.

The rain was ice sickles that fell from the sky
and kept blocking the way of my mystical ride.

The course was a blur but to my surprise,
there were two mascots that rode at my side.

We passed the pied piper on his way to a ball,
in his coach sat a pumpkin ten feet tall.

Across the clouds toward the other side,
sat a jester with a staff a mile high. He broke
up in laughter as he passed me by, and I
waived him farewell from far behind.

We passed lightening steaks that were razor sharp
and ballerinas dancing to invisible harps.
People flying in the mid of the air, we rode right
through them as if they weren't there.
Down below I saw unicorns, They were! I swear,
but they had no horns.

Animals I've never seen before, stepping out of
thresholds that had no doors; flowers that bloomed from
cement in the sky, forbidden to pick, except at night.

This ghost of a tale to my fascination,
is the deepest part of my imagination.

Surely Afraid

Shallow waters peak at sunrise,
rives wind into nowhere.

Tears dry before they touch the ground,
death and silence leaks all around.

Milk and honey aren't fit to eat,
once soured its lost its sweet.

Searching for direction where there is none,
pretending you know, so just falling In line.

A shiny object threatens my life,
a driving force within my sight.

None so admirable, not even one,
that would rescue me from my doom.

This child, not necessarily of any age,
longs to be safe, but is surely afraid.

Tapestry

Crossed and turned under and in,
patterns making non the sense…
A constant effort to reach the end,
as only the master can imagine.

Such as this world we live in,
answers to questions never given.
Details of generations before us,
passed over and held within our trust.

As threads become tattered and torn,
the pictures fades to a vestige worn.
Still, it tells a story with no words,
speaking clearly, it is plainly heard.

Fibers thick and thin,
are the substance of life within.
Depicting more than the eye can behold,
the tapestry of old.

The Last Birth

Born again to this earth,
I take in the breath of life
and tackle the great unknown—
this anomaly they call life.

The earth's wind blows with a
somber rhythm, a tribute to those
who we lost but forgiven.

To the deepest neuron of my mind,
I search for knowledge I left behind
but somehow it seems benign.

As the days pass in rhythmic time,
and the universe turns a page each night,
I realize at my last life's try,
I didn't quite get it right.

And so this time, and my last breath,
I ponder on this life I've led.
Before I close my weary eyes
and pray I see the light—
comes a welcome sign that signifies,
I finally got it right.

The Windy Side

I see transparent stars which
flicker so near and yet so far.
In a glassy milky way,
that leads to where we are.

Open your heart to the moonlight,
drink in its beam of light,
pitch your fear to the windy side,
slip into the silence of this night.

Let us remember this peaceful flight
we took together on that windy side;
the universe reined its dark and light,
we quietly melted into the night's sky.

One and one makes two,
a metaphor of me and you.

Living Dreams Asleep

Dreaming in another life,
while dreaming within the same,
It's all so very confusing,
as I sort the pieces in my brain.

Nuts, bolts and jumbled thoughts,
scatter within my Brainstem knots;
they divide into a collective pool
where sometimes I dream I'm the fool.

A messy puddle of stories not real
turns my thoughts to a haunting ordeal.

What I dream—
I wonder,
is it someday to be,
or is not what I perceive.

Where Is My Love?

Where are you my love?

Soft kisses, so tender so sweet,
whispered in my ear,
your love songs on my cheek,
I'm feeling your presence so near.

The calm of jazz fills the room,
as we dance by the light of a half lit a moon.
You stroke my hair with a tender hand,
I think it is a dream, I never want to end.

By the confines of a blazing fire,
within our private space,
we share the fruit of the vine,
and naturally embrace.

This moment frozen in time,
such a feeling so sublime,
searching endless shores,
to finally look into your eyes.

Where are you my love?
I suppose only time will tell,
I don't know you at all,
but yet, I know you oh so well.

Lost and Void

An Asteroid, lost and void,
till God made you into his toy.
Long ago he gave you birth,
and called your name; Earth.

Oh sun created by God's hand,
giving light into this land,
beware for the time of your demise,
for soon it will be at hand;
a roaring cinder from the future,
will come to make you burn, and whither.
A flash of light, a cosmic rain in the night,
you'll disappear far from our sight.

Oh pretty moon swirl round and round,
the milky way your playground;
your light will dim like a bulb gone bad
and you, will finally fade to black.

Oh stars which blanket all of space,
formed from planets of old,
exploded yourselves in the universe
forming galaxies unknown.

Long ago he formed you all,
but your fate it lies in a fiery ball.

Once long before there was day or night,
long past the light years of time,
a flower bloomed from a lifeless Earth,
forming a magnificent birth.

An architecture before our eyes,
was once but an atom, in the creators eyes.
A concept difficult for mortals to conceive,
twas a lifeless void bearing not even a weed.

CHAPTER 4

ECLECTIC MUSES

Velvet Petals

In a field of thorns a flower so fair,
most unappreciated by her peers;
thus life beginning with her seed,
created by God's own deed.

Beauty spread so wide,
it emanates into the night.

Her velvet petals tucked snug and tight,
into her fortress out of sight.

Tears

Tears of pain come once again,
and make way for tears of joy.

What to say of tears that fall
from infant girls and boys?

A cleansing of the troubled soul,
amidst the sorrow we hold;
it helps us find the truth,
to matters uncontrolled.

Mending fragmented parts of me,
which scatter running free,
though little drops of salted hope,
suddenly, I see.

When I fall from saving grace,
it is only for a season,
till mercy falls in its place
and answers bring me reason.

It's only then, when the waters flow free,
bringing relief that heals a part of me.

Tired Are My Eyes

A glint of sunlight peaks
from a darkened cloud,
as I take down my umbrella—
the rain, she falls in shrouds.

I call to a higher apprise,
my footsteps are yet weary,
none to my surprise;
tired are my eyes.

The silent bits that stir within,
I think of many ways—
of how to set things right
and when to walk away.

I ponder such upon these things,
alas from day to night;
from rain to sun and that between,
still it lingers on my mind.

I seek to find a truth in lies,
but none to my surprise;
tired are my eyes.

No more examples left to follow,
in a haze of no repentance;
who is called to do the deed
for those in need of vengeance?

No rest ye from the pulls within,
until you pause inside;
yet still this burden haunts me—
none to my surprise;
tired are my eyes.

I Awaken to the morning,
to find what's in its midst;
the rested soul can surely see,
a perspective somewhat different.

I open up my thoughts to find,
by my own admittance,
It's the peace we sacrifice;
None to my surprise;
tired are my eyes.

The Tree of Logic

In the tree of logic
bewildered to the bone,
I rise my cup to days of now,
for life's so hard to hold.

In effervescent frolic,
I bend my self-esteem,
to fit the space of time,
that occupies my being.

The essence of a jaded dream,
guided by our will to think,
calls to interaction that,
becomes a preexisting thing.

Windows

Windows from outside the garden,
pure as Eden was created.
Dew is fresh upon my skin,
I miss it now and then.

Flowers kissed the heavens,
trees wave in the wind,
pure as holy water,
drink it with no sin.

The spectrum of the rainbow,
beneath the purple sky,
only for to show her colors,
once in a precious while.

The moon tucks in for a long night's rest,
another day renews.
The sunshine awaits in haste,
while windows fog in morning dew.

Figure of a shadow,
sheltered by a darkened crest,
leaking in the dust filled sand,
the elements regress.

Woven In The Wind

Love woven in the wind,
through warps of time we
catch up with it.

Patience shall cause us to persevere,
tolerance casts wisdom to the air.

Purgatory,
a station of recess,
to sort out the good
and dispose of the rest.

No arbitration at this time,
the God-mind shall aid us to find,
peace and dreams, spirit and soul,
I thank you for what I shall soon know;
the ability to fail, lose or sin…

I'm grateful for your love
woven in the wind.

The Writer

I șit with pen in hand,
await the flow of words—
to paint my work of art,
through my silly, jumbled blurbs.

Once again, my scribbles evolve
from memories and life,
to learn what I seek to know,
and find a way to write.

Write me down on pages,
the deepest, dark designs;
words that flow from the ages,
an abyss developed from my mind.

The pen is sloping downward,
jotting where's and why's;
a menagerie of homeless thoughts
sitting patiently aside.

Meaningless dribble dripping in and out,
from a pen full of black, meandering about.

Words are my stories, that I tell to those who hear,
with everyone it fits— from a laugh to a tear.
My rhetoric and piddle, born of a single thought;
sometimes I write—and sometimes not.

Then...There Was Nothing

There was pursuit at first; notes of endearment,
child's play of stolen kisses and wake-up calls,
a love grows and they give their all.

Love ran deep through the veins of two;
only those two mattered for
there were roses and modest gifts,
treasurers held as gold.

Diners with candles of light,
wine and romance filled the night.
There were words echoing to the depths of their souls,
and passion that carried them to lands unknown.

The touch of his velvet hand, moved slow across her cheek.
Honesty between them grew sacred and discreet.
Conversations of love, life and future tossed to and fro;
Visions relived of the past rekindled a new hope.

First... Love
*Second...*Trust
*Third...*Digression
Forth... Silence
*Fifth...*Weeping
Last...Nothing...

Before The Rain after the Pain

Before the rain,
the sun shed light over flowers
and other living things.

That was... before the rain.

There was warmth, joy, and love.
The morning wakes to a melody of song,
playing over and over as I sang along.

That was... before the pain.

Silently screaming out loud,
the seething rage of thunderous clouds.
Logic falls victim to dissension;
which way to the angels, I cry, and wonder,
what I did—and why.

Once there was peace—now anger.
Unrest, untidy bits of particles haunting my gut.
I scramble to find remission, but there is none.
I flow in and out of my distress,
while sorting out this daunting mess.

One day without a warning, I ran in bitter haste,
as the Lord shouted from above, "repent your harbored hate."

Finally...and with out haste,
I changed the course of what could have been,
a self inflicted fate;

that was... after the pain...

Endless Lines

The mystic marble of beauty,
painted across the sky,
leads me to Imagine,
in a blink of my mind's eye.

Those shapes and lines I can't confine,
only the flow of colors that fall on canvas white.

Thus, follow your mind through space and time,
let illusion be your guide,
to turn your work of endless lines,
to a story without rhyme.

Born to Die: ***Shad***

On a cold autumn night
a child was born,
a life not meant for this world.
Anointed form God, perfect in sight,
but timing of birth was not exactly right.

Struggling for the breath of life,
made you weary and too tired to fight.
A blessed angel born of woman and man,
I believe God called you to be with him.

That fateful night it rained, it stormed,
the first of the season, as if the Earth mourned.

My only son conceived,
after all these years, I still grieve.
I never held you in my arms,
but I loved you with all my heart.

As years pass and life's more defined,
I watch you grow in my mind.
Although it is my private vision,
I'm grateful you live with God in heaven.

Father God

The clouds were my pillows,
as I lie me down to sleep,
before I ride that shooting star
with angels at my feet.

I watch the daylight turn to night,
while riding on majestic wings,
above the clouds of white,
I can almost hear the angels sing.

A journey's filled with feathered sails
upon a dragonfly,
it let me live my fantasy,
through space and father time.

Father God, your universe so great,
a far, the vast horizon lie,
beyond the weightless space.

Creek People

My people rage with thunder;
for the land is tainted waste
of the white man's machines.

My people cry with the rain that flows
through the belly of Mother Earth.

My people dance to the beat of
the drum's rhythm and sing the with the eagles.
Blessed by he, Father of the Four Winds,
the Creek survives to heal the land.

My people are free in their hearts
but imprisoned by greed.
My people live and die in honor.

My people pray to the Creator of Life,
as the smoke rises to this mighty one
on wings of pipes and truth.

My people share freedom through the eternal soul,
and one day meld into the peace
of the Great One's spirit.

Damn Demon

It is said to sew my seeds of life
upon the barren soil,
knowing they would not grow—
it scoffed at my turmoil.

Damn the demon for what it's done,
and has done so very well;
from carnal knowledge ascertained,
its darkened motives were revealed.

Damn the demon full of scorn,
makes my poor heart cry;
it stole away my only hope,
based on subtle lies.

"Why take ye all the Merry sir?"
I asked through tears belied;
"For many damsels envy me,
O maiden Laurelie"...
"But Sir, I only wish for love,
and bear my loved one's pride".

I pled to him in pity,
for mercy so unfitting.
"What profits more than money to let go the
milk and honey?"
"Why ye punish poor lady fair
for I have done no wrong to thee,
and yet you score to punish me?"

His brow did raise through the fiery gaze,
then laughed again as he said,
"For every bit of happiness,
tis sorry I shall shed."

From shores to seas of deepest green,
I shall seek to try again,
and pray to be delivered from,
the ole damned demon's sin.

A Season (for Cindy)

One tiny little tear drop
has fallen to my cheek.
I use my hand to brush it aside—
my integrity is weak.

The candle flickers wildly
to the stillness of the night;
my shadow fades to darknesses
as I blow the flame aside.

Resting on my pillow,
thoughts dance 'round my head,
I pray to him in silence
for the soul now laid to rest.

Thus revealed an answer,
by mediative means—
a quickened thought that came to pass
unto me in a dream.

One precious grain of sand,
amongst the sea of life,
glistens on its very own
into a ray of light.

Every bird that's flown the Earth
has done so for a reason;
not one has lived in vein,
not even for a season.

Circles Broken

Circles broken in patterns unspoken,
the wage loss can't be redeemed.
I cry for my desperate needs...

Trapped in thoughts I can't contain,
tattered memories of love and distain,
exhausted and less shored I've become—

my life has come undone...

No mourners here for a love gone bad;
once crossed that sacred ground,
into the blank of a stone— scarred love
where not a remnant can be found.

My body sure must be alive,
as I fight my own demise.
The path I seek of lesser walk,
I've yet been able to find.

The numbing side the leaver left
takes time to compromise—
time alone and time to be,
and time to realize.

The dark night comes upon me,
the moon shines half its own,
the fog entraps my atmosphere,

and *I, have come undone...*

Medusa Tree

A Blackbird stops his journey,
to rest on angry limbs.
Branches of malcontent,
wave out to the whistling wind.

He preens a feather or two,
to prepare his continued flight.
Skeptically he cocks his head and
piers off to the right.

"Let us Go"
calls a cry from within.

He nodes his head just a bit,
he takes it in his stride,
he closes one small eye,
to analyzes his plight.

"Let us Go"
he hears again.

Victims of this angry tree,
call in discontent.
But Blackbird has no intention,
to take part in this predicament.

"Let us Go"
"Let us Go"

Dodging the perils of this situation,
he lunges to his flight,
and soars the sky in freedom
to his personal delight...

For a Blackbird cares for none but he,
and where he seeks to be,
nor for another's peril,
trapped in a Medusa Tree.

My Last Good-Bye

In this final journey
I hear the fair warning.

A fog of virtue clouds my space,
in and out of this eternal maze.
I trudge this virgin territory,
anticipating, my wait.

Clumps of matter left undone
those matters in stale waters,
that penetrate through my bones;
it seems of less importance,
...as I find myself alone.

Rescinding from this familiar form
into this placid station—yet I do not mourn.
As the time draws near, I lift my heart
to an arc of light—I'm told it's time to
prepare my flight...

To the far most realm of humility,
I'm giving it up to serenity.

I'm lead to the waters of rest,
where the light shall warm my space,
and peace shall be my final bliss.

I Saw Him Die

A rapid bullet meant for anyone,
but it found him.

I saw him die.

His head embraced in my helpless arms,
tears clouded his eyes,
he whispered faintly. “I’m afraid.”

I saw him die.

My grip became tighter. “Hold on my friend”,
I begged. “Please.”

Then…the last breath he exhaled
took his soul, his being—
the essence of a life unfinished,
a story with one less character,
a piece of goodness lost from this world.

The little boy who played Army in the creek.
The young man who met with his first kiss.
The husband who said his good byes to serve.
The dad who never met his son.

I saw him die.

Holding back the tears, my body
ached to cry. I said my final goodbye to
the vision of two warriors invincible,
compadres concurring the matters
of life and childhood dreams, until
that moment of sacrifice— his, mine,
the loss of a brother.

For a moment, the years regressed
to another dimension in time,
relived in a split second—the embrace of
enlisting together - we would concur forever.

I saw him die…. and a part of me with him.

River

The dance of billows swaying,
by your perfect command.
A rhapsody of ripples
leads steady across the land.

Sparkling bright in a perfect moonlight,
under the star— filled night.

Entwining here and there—
that leads to lands of nowhere.

Painted upon your waters,
reflections such as glass,
your journey mapped by time
to a destination vast..

So it Goes

Somehow I lost my friend,
we were pals unto the end.

I drift like a log down stream,
my sleep brings haunting dreams.

Laughter subsided far too soon,
no finish to the song-less tunes,
giggles and whispers gone so soon.

Somewhere back in time,
I can hear our voices chime—
like music never ending,
and a story told with no beginning.

End does end and so it goes;
my ears are deaf and my eyes
now closed.

When you left, I could not go;
it broke my heart my sister soul.

The only sound I hear for now,
is a single tear drop to the ground.

Practical Prose

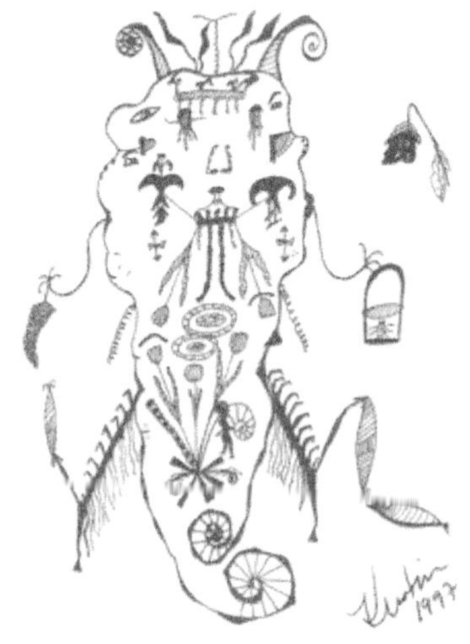

CHAPTER 5

PRACTICAL PROSE

A Curious Situation

This dampness beneath my feet,
sends chills through me of disbelief.
I think I've been here before,
by the familiar locks that bar the door.

Darkness grew here; there is no escape
from my ominous fear that tests my faith.

Afraid of what lurks within the halls,
I feel a strange sensation call.
These walls hold strange graffiti—
marks left from visitors previously.

Ailing floors of cold cement,
are open hotels for lurking varmints.
There are no neighbors of the human race,
or hierarchy to present my case.

I see no escape by visible means,
as I sit and ponder on my deeds.

"FOOL!" a voice calls with impatience
"Behold your curious situation—
you are in a place of revelation,
fitting called "The Station"."

"It is safe from the demising clutches of life,
so put aside your ignorance for a time;
it is not for you to choose or even claim the right."

"Now place your mind to rest,
clear your soul of unwanted guests,
for you will be granted a vision in sight—
but only at the designated time."

A Good Day to Die

As each day passes over and finds its end,
the circle of the tribe congregates to hear
the prophecy and wisdom of the Shaman.

We have brought life to our land and in turn
it has provided food of plenty for the young and old,
but when the light of the moon no longer shines full,
tomorrow's battle will come unannounced,
warriors must call to ancestors asking for victory.

Grandfather, it is a good day to die.

When our flesh leaks from the lead that will fill our bones,
painted faces shall fall like water over mountains.
Some will change in shape and form
to find the derivation of their souls.
White eyes, beware when the ghost dance rise
and the war dance unfolds.

Guns, swords and arrows fly, war is never ending
in a warrior's eyes; braves die, braves fight to preserve
the rivers of life and land of plenty.

Everyday is a good day to die.

As land is sold to a mortgage of death,
with honor and no regrets, the smoke of the pipe
shall rise until the last cloud fades and the buffalo is safe.

Many generations come and go,
the Cherokee stay the same
yesterday, today and yet tomorrow—
and braves will always chant,

Everyday is a Good Day to Die.

A Lover's Analogy

Acid rain fell from your heart one day,
it formed clouds that wouldn't dissipate,
nor even would they fade.
Your silent cries caught my ear,
mingled sadly with old and new tears.
Hallways of memories disappear,
hidden neatly by your fears.

I could not hold you or ease your pain,
for you were so very far away.
I conversed with you by order of meditation,
through a metaphoric dissertation.
We waltzed by the moon's light,
wading in an ocean of glistening tides,
under the stars shining by night.

We shared the price of love,
we melted our minds with the Father God and Son.
Through the windows of our eyes,
a symbolic reflection of crimson and white,
does cover you in his purest light
and leads you back to the road of life.
A cumbersome road with long winding turns,
but nonetheless a lesson learned.

Finally, when the tide of love,
washes where loneliness was,
you will build a bridge to replace those walls.

Again and Again

As another year falls to the depths of turmoil and travail,
I long to see a beacon of rainbows and goodwill.

A tripod of experience fades to black and amber,
leaving memories of life I cannot quite remember.
Dreams change, some repeat—
I'm a pawn on a chessboard waiting for defeat.

New births, new deaths go on forevermore,
souls try again to get it right,
to even up the score.

Tired to My Soul (for TRH)

My heart is now half gone,
my journey to unfold,
the unknown path ahead,
makes me tired to my soul.

Your love does still surround me
though death took you away,
I wonder how I'll make it
through, the lonely rest of days.

Tired of seeking answers
to questions I do not know,
tired of the pain,
that death does now unfold.

I'm flooded in my thoughts,
as my mind replays the years,
the happiness we shared,
now branded in my tears.

What greater love than this,
the spirit gives us all,
your walk with God complete,
as his angel you've been called.

You spent your days in learning,
and your time in teaching all,
the years upon this earth,
lead you to listen to your call.

Now do the work of teaching,
on a higher plain of truth,
what every soul doth seek
is now what you will do.

In all that you have taught me,
the knowledge I've abound,
but now it's time to lay your ashes,
into the dust filled ground.

With memories and tears,
and sorrow to the bone,
I say my last goodbye,
to the greatest love I'd ever known.

At Denny's

I watched them as they sat together,
so far, they were from one another.

She with cherry colored lips,
his eyes seemed a thousand miles from bliss.

A quick glance to acknowledge her there,
then fell back in to his sublime nowhere...

Consider Love

Love knows no…
boundaries
color
race
nor age,
it brings only homage our way.

Consider love,
now and then,
and enigma without end.

Captured

A host of thoughts blaze through my brain,
of neurons firing a hazy maze,
interrupting my quiet sublime,
speaking all at once,
and at the same time.

My unconscious conscious,
is working over time,
enlightening my soul,
across space and time.

Definition

I hear a whisper in my ear,
a thought which spreads through the atmosphere.
It draws no line between good and evil,
but yet is undefined.
It is a strange definition, a matrix of such,
between reason and rapture; I need a bit of luck.

Thoughts commingle within my flesh,
and I shiver at what seems less than my righteousness.
Knowledge gained from this prison called my mind
leaves me wondering how to edit without blacking out the
lines.

I Am…

a mantra, repeating through this vast universe.

I am

a void passing beneath the highways of time.

I am

grief, and have cried for those who fed me their lies.

I am

breached by a trust, leaving me to float in darkness.

I am

a love that forgives.

I am

an island, true to myself,

which is what I would consider,

the greatest of wealth.

In This Particular Man's World

I saw two lovers kissing behind the oak tree,
hiding from the open so no one could see.
Not a word did they speak, trying to be discreet.

They radiated love,
caressing one another's face
with tenderness, dignity, and grace.

Embraced in their secret world together,
hoping no one would disturb them ever.

One fair-haired and lanky, the other stocky and tan;
this unlikely couple, like so many there are,
only seek to be equal and open to all.

Life after Life

There, a revelation of information,
I see in visions of my reformation.
I emerged from the jail of submissive selfishness
and continue to work toward my righteousness.

I gain knowledge by many a means,
In every existence my soul is still me.
The revelation is never the same,
So I come back to learn,
but not in vain.

I've come to the end of this life,
ready to take my usual flight.
Breaking free, it's time to ascend,
to get my orders and live again.

In The Corporate Bed

Chains clatter while voices echo
in vengeance and sorrow.
In a cool mist, I ride the invisible waves
between reality and doom.

I am castigated by
the bombardment of nonsense
and the constant circle
of musing indignities.

Hacking away, chipping at the stones
that represent freedom
of deliverance from abashment,
has yet become my salvation or refuse.
Still, I witness the maze of these
non-virtuous clock watchers
and their boring summations
of meaningless clamor.

Daily, I fight my way
through the corporate digest of fools and charlatans
who seem to all be in search
of their foolish philosophical apotheosis.

Unsettled

Unseen matter haunts my dreams,
with visions of transparent souls
that seem so real to me.
They cry at night from their lonely graves,
begging for mercy to clear their names.

Aimlessly, they circle around,
in dimensions to which
they are hopelessly bound.

At times I hear those mournful moans,
of disparity, sorrow, and confinement unknown.
They beckon my help and reprieve,
but I'm unable to lend a hand
or aid them in their need.

Dark Side

The dark side emerges less bright,
through naked lenses of reddish light.
Raw horror, puddles of blood,
lead to innocence raptured,
absence of love.

The pit opens to emerge its pitch,
that spews like vomit upon the naked spirit.

Draped in his unholy mask,
the dark prince plants his kiss,
with baneful venom in his midst,
that destroys its victim to nothingness.

Beware of vapors that wind and waver,
disdainful deeds, compel the demon's savor.

When prayer falls still and morality dies,
pictorial truths turn to flagrant lies;
perception cannot penetrate, nor feel insipid faith.
In darkness is stored falsified comfort,
in hopes of defeating the angel's trumpet.

A ride not worth the vehicle's trouble,
the serpent beguiles ever so subtle

When the apocalypse rises east of the moon,
and the stars who gamble their fate too soon,
fail to shine in the enigmatic tomb,
then perhaps our faith has fled too soon…

Roses Die

On a bed I lie with petals
of roses at my feet,
abundance of red,
a dozen I think.

Velvet and lovely,
I feel compassion,
for this delicate flower
now void of action.

Once seeds that floated in the wind,
etched in the tides of time,
until they give up an earthly life.

Nature Interrupted

A million stars still shine
from the cold night's sky,
amongst the moon and her glory
that knows not of time.

The blazing sun now thrusts its rays
through an atmosphere
on the cusp of decay—
brought to you by
technology today.

Creatures from everywhere
bow to this imminent justice,
that grows distinct
with great reluctance.

Led we are by a blinded eye,
while the storm grows stronger,
they continue to deny.

The legacy of this tired old king
will be recorded as a blemish on history.

Ship's Grave

Wooden shrine protected
by thrones of invisible eves.
Stench that lingers—
promises reveal no truths, only still;
pillar of salt, pirate of ghost ship,
once shiny perfection,
now a remanent,
a ruin of destruction.
Ancient secrets abide,
silence dwells deep inside.

A cold monument lies encased.
The spirit moves not—
in the depths of their grave,
Hulls green with moss,
withered down, and forever lost.

Wake Up Call

Each morning I set my internal clock
to the light of day,
which forces coherency to seep
through my unwilling bones.
My eyes bolt open,
charging like warriors against a new battle.

Once again, I'm expected
to fulfill obligations that force me to face
the imminent fate of my future.
I wonder if loneliness is learned,
or if it is a by-product of poverty,
heaped upon us through
unrealistic expectations of conditional life.

Those miniature rays of hope
are intensely grasped between
clenched knuckles and tightly bound hands.
Layers of dreams are peeled back
like pages to forgotten chapters—
read and re-read, but not retained.

It becomes astutely apparent each day
that the road leading to hope
has detached itself from my desires.

Caught in a sphere of never-ending confusion,
I watch my childhood dreams,
carved from fairytales and hope,
explode back into the universe
from which they first came.

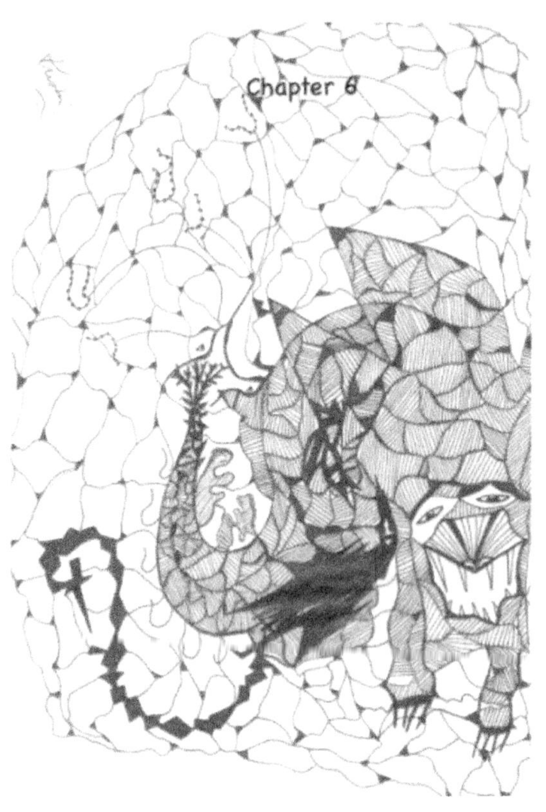
Chapter 6

CHAPTER 6
DETOUR

Vacation

I left to tomorrow,
to stumble through today,
holding on to sanity—
help me find my way.

I step inside this circle,
excuse myself from this day,
my mind's working overtime,
without the extra pay.

My night vacation rolls around,
it never comes too soon.
I close my eyes and crack a smile,
then begin my snooze.

Here I lie half asleep,
counting the dogs and sheep,
jogging through the atmosphere,
seemingly fancy free…

Swinging from the stars,
hanging by the moon,
as long as I can sleep,
it's what I live to do…

Shoot the Beast

Shoot the beast, warriors of war,
sport of profit; game of gain.
Shallow graves dug deep,
earth spews them from her belly
as if counting sheep.

The good die young in worthless wars
for reasons quite unknown.
Seek the beast, shoot the beast—
all in the name of peace.

Armchair warriors play their chess,
while silently orchestrate the mess.

Deals of trade and bad advice,
all sewing sacrifice—of innocent people,
their homes and land, the hour of doom is now at hand.

Stalk the prey, lest anger be held at bay,
angel of death, walk with thee
unto thy lonely grave—
fearing it be a moment away.

Shoot the beast,
till the last tear's shed,
and guns and swords
be put to bed.

I'm Torn

I'm searching for my faith,
nothing seems too real,
I'm going through the motions
that I can't seem to feel.

I've been stripped of my dignity,
I'm staring at the wall,
my eyes are closed to motion as
I'm watching myself fall.

I don't want your sympathy,
it leaves me empty and afraid,
just leave me to my mourning,
so I can hide away.

I've been the perfect picture,
framed in what I'm supposed to be,
but I've wasted so much time now,
it's torn me from reality.

Defamed to the bone,
my shame is hard to bear,
taken all I have till there's
nothing left to share.

I thought perhaps a glimmer left,
but see no end in sight,
there is no more left in me,
I've given up the fight.

My hope is scattered on the floor,
I cry for this remiss.
I swallow up my pride
and drink this cup of bitterness.

I'm torn and I'm broken,
I lie in my distress,
for nothing is left from this;
I guess that's all there is.

Time Passages

Time passages to a new tomorrow,
the sunrise of yesterday, it borrows,
and leaves the day without a sorrow.

Shine, O' harvest moon,
from early evening's bloom,
for the next sunrise
does come too soon.

These Things

Awaken sweet desire,
rekindle that old flame,
let old regrets die to the wind,
let ties unbroken remain.

Renew a life to smiles,
and flirt with new desires...
Love as one, grow old as two,
seal it tight with the vows renewed.

A soul to bond with...
A heart to rejoice with...
A companion to converse with...
one to laugh and cry with...
Sharing, giving make a life worth living.

The Gift

Into your eyes I behold,
a feeling I've never known.
None so strong, nor comforting
and none so close to home.

I'm amused at the timing,
unexpected but yet exciting,
A strange connection to my soul—
You are the mate for which
I've searched this globe.

Somewhere beyond the sun,
is a land worthy of love,
where there is no greater gift,
then two joined as one.

The Story Without End

The paper has yellowed with age,
and its ink now faded away.
I can barely read the written lines,
but when I close my eyes,
they become clear in my mind.

Pen and ink have not changed,
for life as I once knew,
there's only the space in which I am contained,
far beyond the sky of blue.

Each waking day, a effort I make,
in search of a thought,
to find the words I want to say.

Home is past the sun,
where everything melds into one,
and visions of hope fill the heavens above,
with family and friends who have since passed on.

Tables of Age

If it were you and not I,
would you search illusions in time?
There'd be no sentiment to disrupt,
nor penitence to give up.

Such bane I feel as the creeping of years
steals the pleasure of youth, leaving lines and tears.

Is life a cruel, unusual game, that is not
much more than chance to change?
What rules written must we break,
when weighing our tables of age?

Experience I confess, but you at yours,
have none the less.
You and I, we choose,
the ultimate risk of being bruised,
and I will render to the end,
a gamble worth the wager I'm in.

Perhaps a future lasting forever,
a never-ending pleasure,
or, for some, a torment, when the past is
present—and that is the time it is measured.

I welcome not a pending hell…
but pray for the love that has been felt.

The Cognate Corpses

Ergo this love today,
for nothing ever stays the same.

Fury, red with vengeance,
former love, viper pawn,
trident weapon, desire spawned—
this cognate corpse is moving on.

Gutters formed from salty veins,
protruding claws in miry clay.
Snatch the innocence from the night,
under a moon raging fire and light.

Tainted rain weakness whisper,
heart rotting in this hemisphere,
of bleak compost and dismay,
where broken bones decay,
smoldering back to dust,
from whence they surely came.

If Only

If only, I could feel the sunshine without rain,
touch the heavens without refrain,
and dance upon the mountain tops
in a shadow of silvery mirrored moon,
just one more time again.

If only, I could love without the pain,
feel the passion flowing through my veins,
and the excitement of a spirit dance to the rhythm
of drums and chants, around a fire aglow,
I would sing the songs of my tribes from the days of old.

If only, I knew the secret of peace
where all were one and hatred ceased.

Remember 911

Angry screams, demons chant,
souls sold cheap, spirits trapped.

Hidden beneath the ear is spun,
robes of fear provoked by one.

Led astray in dangerous lands,
destruction caused by evil hands.
Rulers reign the captive tribes,
and preach their hatred based on lies.

Women betrayed, cover their faces—
tormented and taken, they fall from grace.

A creed of jihad breeds the unjust,
a twisted faith sacrificed in death;
a hollow victory only once,
until judgment swallows and spits them out.

A philosophy that, in the end,
cannot survive or win,
but will wreak its havoc until then.

The Haunts

Sometimes I hear the haunts
disturbing my dreams,
and illusions of those long deceased,
trying to be seen.

They cry from their lonely graves,
begging for mercy to clear their names.
Aimlessly, they circle around,
in a dimension of which they are hopelessly bound.

I hear their moans of woe
and try hard to console,
but their sorrow and confinement
is not in my control.

The bodiless entities roam in such stress,
searching endlessly for their final rest.

Rhythm

The paper has yellowed with age,
and its ink is nearly faded away.
I can barely read the written words,
but when I close my eyes,
they become quite clear.

Pen and ink have not changed,
only the space in which I take.
Life as I once knew,
has far been passed it's cue.

Systematically, each waking day,
a concerted effort I make,
in search of a new adventure,
to find the words I want to say.

Miles of empty highways,
weeds and sticks along the way—
kicking rocks and picking stones,
there's somewhere a place carved in time
where I can call my own.

I close my eyes to see eagles soar
and the waves on
the distant ocean's shore,
and amber waves on mountain tops;
I never see rainbows anymore.
Yet grateful for my fruitful mind,
where I imagine what I need—
a place to escape reality,
or simply plant the seed.

Roll

We can only move forward
if we are willing to embrace the past…
We must live until
our breath takes its last…
After this, what is next?
Just a plain and simple roll of the dice.

Meditative Intellections

This station is empty,
so I sit contemplating;
a conscience filled with empty rags,
fragments of baggage lost in a world
of confusion and foiled emotion.
Habitual notions lead me down
a dead-end street of smoldering ashes...

People, people...

YOU CAN'T GIVE WHAT YOU DON'T FEEL.
YOU TAKE WHEN IT FEELS GOOD.
YOU CAN'T MAKE YOURSELF LOVE
UNTIL YOU LOVE YOURSELF.
YOU CAN'T TEAR DOWN A WALL
IF YOU WANT TO REMAIN
IN ITS ISOLATED FREE FALL.

What drives me to a place of emotional tides,
pulling me in and out?
Is there a balance to this coming about?
LIARS AND CHARLATANS
ALL HAVE THEIR PLACE
IN THE ABYSS ETERNAL,
Far from Grace.

Power is not given but taken.
Power taken destroys the innocence
and devours that which first started out sincere.
Power becomes the monster of destruction
to anyone in its path.

BIDE YOUR TIME
AND FIND YOUR PEACE.
RELAX IN THE KNOWLEDGE—
WHAT WILL BE, WILL BE.

Then

Beyond the heavens,
beyond the stars,
far beyond the seas,
I'm searching for my spirit
within the ranks of me.

Peace is love; happiness and joy
are the ingredients that flow from it.

Then there is caring—
Then there is sacrifice—
Then there is giving—
then… there is love.

Microscopic Control

It's hideous how a microscopic
cell can gain control
by a chemical induced
from one tiny team player,
in a pattern of chromosomal life forms
born from the same energy source.

Redundant how history repeats—
from the inner circle
to the least of all creation;
rot, giant, sculled, hidden, festers, explodes—
those microscopic entities out of control.

Choices

I've made choices of angels
and choices of not,
and the choices of not,
I've easily forgot.

Choices of angels
were quite clear—
in the face of darkness,
I've nothing to fear.

Choices have brought me
heartache and pain,
many I've made,
have been quite in vain.

Hear The Beginning

I'm caught in a dark clamor,
of colors and fibers
that meld in a strange manner.

I am tumbling back to creation
and the birth of a star's formation;
imploding with information,
and forming life with anticipation...

There in clouds of thunder,
it's the heavens boasting
of its perfect wonder.
God smiles upon the deed,
and all is well in eternity.

My Fair-it-y

I ask by what means do you measure,
fairly, sincerity, and practical pleasure?

Think it out clearly, with no open plea,
for the takers—they wait patiently.
Life rarely casts us fair game;
it couples with disparity and shame.

Those who lean to honesty,
don't strain yourself searching aimlessly,
for much is wrong with well-meaning givers,
and promises made by insincere fibbers.

Lavish each day
one at a time,
and look at the world
through kaleidoscope eyes.

Happiness is the purest of joys,
misery is but another poor choice.

I Gave My Love

I gave love, part heart, part soul;
I gave my love wisdom
to help him grow old.
I gave my love the goodness inside of me,
I gave my love the joy of how love can be.

I gave my love the morning
so crisp and clean,
I gave my love no memories
to haunt a part of me.

I gave my love my all,
my everything—
my love gave to me,
little to nothing.

Jumbled Nonsense

I run from the stares
of a revelation sought after
by echoes of lying alliances,
unholy participation—
jilted by the prospects
of the never-ending chapters
that float in a time warp
of thereafter's.

There is no triumph
for a union of derelicts
who work to spread disbeliefs
and needless dread…
The corruption in defaced grace,
in the end,
steals our peace.

Justice for those who serve religion—
beware not to lose the real vision.
There is truth in good decision;
do not part from the vision.

Angels sing glory to those who hear,
because the chaos below is hard to endure.
Through jumbled nonsense and disbelief,
peer deep into what is right to seek.

RED

Oh lovely red candle,
before you were lit,
strong was the mast
of your mighty wick.
Born you were
to fire and flame,
that cast your spoils
into the wind.

Flame

How many times
can you burn,
before your flame dims?
Like man; burn slow, burn fast,
but never long do you last.

When?

When will I ever learn past
the wisdom I've duly earned?
When will I ever believe
my own observations
and convictions I've conceived?

Shadows

Shadows reflect a latent image,
you can catch them everywhere
walking here and there,
until they disappear...

The Tunnel of Light

We are born through a tunnel of light,
fear prompts the first salty tear,
exposing us to a cold world at first sight.

We learn to reach with wanting hands
and gestures that reveal our commands.
Each day brings a lesson, good or bad,
but we learn to adjust, and sometimes laugh.
When we die, we fall back through the tunnel of light,
and are taught our last lesson—*how to die.*

When Did Christmas Die?

I hate Christmas these days,
it's become a mockery, a play on a stage.
Lines of people everywhere I see,
all so in a hurry to quench their need.

It is not the search for something new,
it is the soul which we should seek to renew.
It's not games and food to eat till you pop,
nor eating again until you drop.

Where are the carols that were sung so dear?
Where is popcorn strung in sincere?

Christmas is an exhausting time,
we should be resting, leaving stress behind.

It is not about cooking nor greed,
it is wishing all on Earth Godspeed.
Grateful and kind will give us peace of mind,
but all that has been lost in time.

Remember Christ and His sacrifice,
the Son of God who gave His life.
I hate Christmas these days—
it has turned into a never-ending maze.

Pity

Society breeds self-centered creatures,
pathetic and non-pleasing teachers.
For those who will never taste
honest and prudent ways,
nor the sweet nectar of grace,
it shall slip by and fall to waste.
Pity…

When the days turn telluric,
and hours become misaligned,
judgment will stand tall to the test of time,
and those who seek may rarely find.
Pity…

Mask

The heart is a magnet
that draws my spirit to somber depths.
A mask of emotion is hard to accept.
I piece together in my mind
a reason love can be so unkind.

It can be a gentle flow
to a destination unknown,
or a stagnant pond sitting all alone.

I weep at times when love covers me;
I feel I'm in a place of make-believe.
If only it could live forever,
but it lasts only moments to never.

I watch the demon try to steal it away,
helpless I feel, as I lie awake.

My mask is my fortress in which I escape,
but I'm cold and alone until the end of days.
For love is a mask we all wear at times,
until it leaves us looking behind.

Sometimes I feel like a withered leaf
falling aimlessly from the mother tree,
then on to the ground where death is earned—
my remains crumble, back to Earth.

Fear

Fear is an illusion
we don't always choose,
when reality presents us
with an uncertain muse.

Fear is learned from early days
of what seems real, through a foggy haze.

Fear is the devil,
it lies and survives,
it plays on our minds
leaving no place to hide.

Fear is something you feel,
but it's only illusion appearing real.

Rebel

Stir in the night,
shiver by moonlight,
the rebel rests not—
it hides out of sight.

Fall from grace, bury burdens,
and slay the dragons to waste.
Heroes of another fold
stand strong and bold.

Raise the gun of fantasy and fire,
then run until you've fulfilled your desire.

As long as forever, rebels die,
and finally leave their guns behind.

The Paradox Within

Something sustaining, far from our reach,
is a destiny we must seek,
yet the mountain is steep
and the valley quite deep.

What is this paradox I see,
where I seek to find the inner me?
I can't find this soul I seek,
though the signs are quite unique.

Again, my search falls out of tune,
and a fortress rises like a piteous moon.
I think there is no end to my query,
for the journey has become so weary.

If loneliness is a virtue,
what could possibly be the issue?
An isolation of one,
to wither away until there is none?
What road do we travel to our final rest,
after this life and on to death?
And where does a spirit hide,
when it wants to find a way back to life?

Signs

I've been kissed by a hush
that never touched.
I've been barely kissed by lips,
in an almost brush.

I've felt the sensations,
the stares and flirtations,
but like a dream when you wake,
it's not real but fake.

I run from turbulent tides,
that bends my spirit and steals my pride.
I'd rather not be kissed,
than experience a miss.

The Final Walk

I have reached with wanting hands
beyond the fullest of moons.
My soul has danced in the darkest night
until my dreams came true.

Dreams of promises by the angels' light,
tossed around a silver lining
beneath the clouds so bright.
Upon the grass glazed over,
among newly fallen leaves,
I've journeyed around the Earth
with blessings of "Godspeed."

In such times of sadness,
my head has bowed to pain,
then came from there another part,
which circles past me once again.
My tears have called in silence
to a hundred thousand names,
written on the scrolls of time
for ancients to proclaim.

I've walked the sands of crystal white
and dined with kings and queens,
but have yet to find the answers
to questions that remain.

For wisdom comes
from gathered knowledge gained,
and joy is what we make it
within our own domain.
In the last of this journey,
I seek my final walk—
to freedom that will lead me
far past the mountaintops.
There, in the midst of a gentle rain,
this vessel sheds its last remains,
fulfilling the heavenly promise
when I speak my Father's name.

Sweet Distain

Distasteful darlings of the night,
prudent charmers of the daylight,
fondled by the pride of pretense,
but the Master makes the dollars and cents.

Decadent derelicts boastful vagabonds,
self center maniacs, seek more and more
until the rip has fully torn.

Suck it up, breath it in and may
the boozers and sinners repent.
Waste them all in a river of honey,
spilling over with greed of money.

Jesters who sit on the edge of life,
looking for entertainment of delight,
find but only sweet distain,
born from yesterday's remains.

You to Me (for JMR)

None has loved me as you do,
for a flood of rainbows surround you.

Love flows from your heart and sweet divine,
the pours of colors circle through your light.

I am lucky to be me, to be so loved by thee.

CHAPTER 7

MOMENTS AND MATTERS

Take a Moment

When you think you can't find yourself,
dashing through life will never help.
The day is gone before your eyes,
and you've accomplished little in this day of life.

Listen to one bird sing.
Breathe the fragrance
of a flower you can't name.
Watch a child at play,
and take a moment to seize the day.

Step in the footprints left in the sand,
and ponder the path at hand.
The cross is not yours to carry—
He took that with love and courage.
He is but a thought away,
as are the angels who bring the new day.
Not all days need be the same
if you ask for peace to lead the way.

Love in a Life

One day the aura dims,
it withers in the wind;
the cruel evolution now thus begins
to tear at the balance within.

Alas the spirit moves not;
the corpse lie dormant but nigh forgot.
In a dark filled room there stirs not a breath,
or a vacant whisper, for there is none left.

When the dance of the love once filled the room,
the chatter died and the life consumed.

Abundant Love

In death we pass not away, just on.
A kind heart will be remembered,
a familiar smile embraced,
not in the body with which it was encased,
but in the legacy of the you
who left without a trace.

Love in much abundance
before it is too late,
never fear to show
your kindness and your grace,
for it will pass the universe,
far beyond this place.

We walk by rivers of gold
and lakes of jasper stone,
the light so white and bright
will guide us to our final home.
Those we left behind
and those who dwell alone,
often will remember
the smiles and abundant love.

Can't

Can't sort out the rubble
of the matter and its trouble,
of wasted triumphs and shallow deeds
of those elected who have taken our very needs.

Ancient Story

Middle age has come to call,
it flew past me like summer to fall.

Silky flowing hair, rose colored lips
and at the body so fair,
sadly the rainbows have disappeared.

My porcelain skin is turning to stone,
but at least I'm not alone.

That is the price of growing old,
the ancient story forever told.

The one rare prize that comes with this,
is wisdom and a bit of bliss.

Testament

I cried a thousand tears in those days.
I cried for the lost and abandoned souls,
for children who craved love,
and for happiness I'd known so little of.

I walked down many roads
and hiked across countless highways
that led nowhere,
in my search for forgotten yesterdays
and departed tomorrows.

My last lucky penny,
carelessly tossed
in a dried-up wishing well,
left me with an eerie chill
as an old memory and me did meet,
beneath a dormant sunshine of peace.

I hopped on the invisible train of glory
and rode through a purple haze of destruction.

My body tempered,
my mind unassembled;
daylight slid into the midnight hour.
A numb reality reared its ugly head,
and the cells in my brain began to die,
one by one.

I found myself alone—
destination, unknown.

Emotion

I write it all down on paper,
I think on it and visit the facts over and over again.
Tears stain my poem, they smear the ink
until the words are unreadable and curse my name.

Emotion… this autocratic king—
grand master of all,
big brother, the enemy, my enemy—remains.

Emotion runs deep, builder of fort, infiltrates me.
In seconds it constructs its great city
amongst vessels within the flow of my blood,
carefully tempering a foundation
around the beating of my heart;
dark art; it has embedded
a remote to my thoughts,
and with a flip of the internal switch
it shuts and locks the door to my soul.

Emotion, erosion, explosion—the enemy.
It reckons me, sums me in like a protocol of death.
Emotion, the enemy, it barters off every cell,
every speck of energy, every breath—
emotion, my enemy, imparted in me till death.

Passion save me,
emotion enslaves me,
rushing in like the lava of a great volcano,
destroying everything in its path, stirring my wrath.

Nuke these thoughts from within and free me again.

Emotion; enemy.

Escape at Sea

Where is my ocean breeze that brushed my cheek,
and fell gently to my feet?
Why do I cry for the things that I can't see,
and why do they cause me such defeat?

The ocean is angry and stealing my summer eve;
the moon shadowed by the darkened clouds,
as the storm settles in, and brings me to my knees.

The rage grows bigger and the sands begin to streak,
the waves become monsters
that swallow the distant island peaks.

I pray for my lord to wash my tears into the ocean deep,
for the sea is vast with many secrets to keep.
I come to the water to find my peace,
and ponder the burdens fallen to me.

I don't run, I don't hide,
for my soul just lets it all happen this night.
I think of so many things that have come and unto my life,
and how many times my broken heart has again, come alive.

I try to escape this dream-like state,
to give my mind a welcome break,
but this circle of thought is hard to escape.
Show me mercy and grace,
and take me to a better place.

Did my soul choose this life of mine,
and the mountains I am forced to climb?
How can my spirit align, to the lessons I've survived?
And if the soul shall never die,
I'll return as another to this earthly life,
with more lessons to fall upon me, until I get it right.

I Heard a Voice (The Prince of Peace)

I was feeling rather down one day,
when I fell into a sleep,
my conscious in an empty state,
I met the Prince of Peace.

I heard a voice of wisdom
in the midnight of the hour,
a faintly spoken whisper,
but one of princely power.

"People who depend on you
for service you are to render,
it would serve the greater good,
if you did it all with splendor."

Then he looked into my eyes,
as if I were transparent,
and left me with this thought
that soon became apparent:

"Take a trip within yourself
and ride it all the way,
the truth is but a moment
before it starts to fade.
Take it to the limit,
learn something every day,
your conscience will abide with you
and wipe the fear away."

I woke up shaking in my sheets
and jumped right out of the bed.
Instead of feeling down,
I felt renewed instead.

I called my love and told him
what happened in the night,
and changed my situation
based upon my spiritual flight.

I told him:
"I'm looking for life within myself to ride it all the way,
and take it to the limits, where I'll never be afraid."

City of Bones

Beneath the wreckage of rocks and sand,
lies a city of bones scattered amidst the land.
Ghosts do haunt the dwellings there, roaming
over and over in great despair.

The search for something
they appear to have lost,
flitter aimlessly as they must.
Not did they know death entered the gate,
giving in to an existence of a never-ending wait.

Wonder and wander, it is taken to task,
yet still there is no one to conversely ask.
Tempered dreams lived over and again,
the road often traveled by souls lost to sin.

Searching and searching without measure of time,
from an endless dimension of curves and winds.

Should purpose someday be emphasized,
and a sudden epiphany arise,
perhaps at the very time,
the haunted soul may close its weary eyes.

Highways of Regret

The highways of regret,
haunt my muddled mind,
pleasure passes quickly
before my very eyes.

Waves are ever breaking,
like thunder in the rain,
Leaves are ever falling
like the tears we cry in vain.

Crossing

Tossing and turning, I'm falling fast it seems;
I'm seeing through a looking glass,

I'm in and out of consciousness,
and almost out of breath.

Turmoil laced with peace—
I can't let go, I can't release.

My stomach is in knots,
before my eyes dance a thousand spots.
My feet are going numb,
my hands and legs don't feel too strong.
My life appears before me,
like a movie set on high speed.

Everything I've ever done,
I'm purposely being shown.
The end is the beginning,
as I see a bright light spinning.

My fear fades away,
and love surrounds my space.
I'm crossing to another side,
where there are no more tears to cry.
Where love is in every breath I take,
and joyful songs are filled with grace.

Bridge of Fragile Means

Oh bridge of fragile means,
where memories do pine,
over rivers which turned to stagnant ponds,
wasted from passage of time.

I close my eyes and visions
show a monument so fine,
where horse and buggy rolled over it,
to get to the other side.

Oh bridge once fresh and new,
now tattered weathered wood,
the years of those who passed,
have worn you out from wheels and foot.

What promises in the moonlight were made,
swaying to and from?
A lover's kiss so sweet and bliss,
evolved to careless unknowns.

Lives swept under your pillars
with secrets decayed,
now resting deep within your bowels,
silenced the hearts enraged.

Girders and rails in perfect rhyme,
once standing erect and sublime,
far reaching past eternity—
a moment left behind.

Begin Again

Melodies change, atoms rearrange,
creating other forms—born different but the same.

Life begins again, from dust of withered bones,
retracing indelible footprints from souls so long ago.

Each generation borrows
the stories from days of old,
names we don't remember
and legacies we'll never know.

The Earth is damp with fallen dew
from hundreds of years ago—
recycled rain gives drink to trees
which found new places to grow.

As seeds scatter in the wind,
the circle of life still flows,
and miracles we witness
remain a mystery unknown.

Energy leaves the dying host when the last breath shall end,
the spirit which never dies looks for rebirth again.

The next in line inherits the right of passage through,
falling into a formless maze, taking what we've learned to do.
Thus some poor used-up souls,
now buried in tombs with unmarked stones,
are apparitions forever wondering
what became of their dust and bones.
When will it end, and what final recycling bin will I end up
being in?

Vagrant

Another lonely day, barely just begun,
my hands deep in pockets,
my toes are feeling numb.

Gather round the barrel, the fire burned out fast,
cinders in the air turn to molten ash.
Street lights just went out I woke up before the dawn
standing on the edge of nothing, where did I go wrong?

It's been longer than a year since my dreams fell to my feet,
from my cozy carpet window to the windy naked street.

They say as fate would have it—well, this faded shirt and me,
living in the shadow of the man I used to be.
It cuts me to the bone and haunts me to my grave,
I feel like half a man with nothing left to say.

Don't throw me any pity from your big black Cadillac,
I don't need your token sympathy to get me off my back.

For every man time forgot, there's a story in his eyes—
come sit and listen, it just might make you wise.
Picking up the pieces from the shadows in the air,
remnants of my life are scattered everywhere.

Hello, goodbye—morning turns into night,
wish I was anywhere but here, I've lost my will to fight.

Hello, goodbye—

I can't seem to get it right, I miss my home,
I miss my life; no one gives a damn if I live or die.

Hello, goodbye.

Through a vagrant's eyes. (a poem and a song)

Another Mountain

In the valley I walk a daunting pace,
in anticipation of my journey of faith.
Ahead of me is another mountain,
with all its beauty and grace;
I've seen it in my dreams—
the very same mountain,
in the very same place.

Winding roads of dirt and dips,
hiding its trails of experience.
I gather up those memories,
and take them home with me.
I have many hours in which to think,
and many days to ponder my mistakes.
I long for a moment of rest,
as my soul aches my regrets.

I've searched for answers
on this mountain in which I've claimed,
above the purple majesty
and its amber waves of grain.

Inside the thunder, trying to catch a glimpse
of knowledge from somewhere
which surely must exist.
It's time for my journey to begin—
the one which will never end.

The Last Lullaby

Melodic harmony passes through my lips,
seems like eons ago.
Promises made one to the other,
un-kept in the long haul.

One moment in time,
re-lives years of our lives;
but for every little smile,
there were two times that we cried.

Surreal warmth runs through my bones,
a familiar security I grew to know,
why did we feel the need to let go?

Jumbled emotions in tumultuous times,
devotion quickly set aside, my heart now
drenched in why.....your memory burned
in my mind.

These words are my gift to you; may you
carry them the rest of your life,
my emphatic love and concern,
spoken in this, our last lullaby.

Memories of You

I walk by the water alone
and watch the dust
kick up the shuffle from my feet.
I feel the breeze chill my bones,
and my insides shiver.

Thunder cracks,
the ground swallows my Earth around me,
and my loneliness is magnified
to the depths of my soul.
The night so black
that the nothings are consumed
by a space that never ends.

The moon is a painted pie tin,
reflecting rays that fade with a blink.
The sun shines, then the rain tumbles
to mask my tears of miss.

There is a haunting in my heart
that pulls and digs at my very being.

My colors have turned to black and white,
and my world is lost
within the memories of you.

Where Angels Soar

Where Angels soar I'll find my way
on this bountiful flight through space;
far above the clouds and rain—
simplicity again.

Before my soul, so much unknown,
and formless spirits surround me
in this transitory home.

From where I write this, my emotions find trouble.
My hand does quiver, and my pen does fumble.
Many moons will come and go
until my wisdom finds its constant flow.

I must let go the meaningless blame,
and learn to live again;
another form, another mind,
perhaps another time.

Each lifetime we wonder—
will it be our last,
or will we have to live again
our mistakes from all our pasts?

Jekyll & Hide

What is this feeling I hold so tight,
and refuse to let go from my sight?

Discord threatens my heart,
there are people around me speaking,
but they're so far apart.

I desire to listen but not to abide,
my senses seem perplexed inside.

I dare not retreat, I dare not hide,
I dare not show what's on my mind.

A twisted dimension is where I reside,
I wear it all well—my Jekyll and Hide.

Warned I was, and listened not,
the voices got louder and then they stopped.

Complain I cannot, for this bed I did make,
but the punishment is hard to take.

A Vampire Cries

How long must I roam these nights,
searching and stalking
the innocent and unsuspecting?
This curse of a thousand years dictates my being,
and I, the slave, must obey the hideous demands
the immortal body craves.

Eternal damnation is the only destiny
for which my future holds.

If I myself could muster the nerve,
I'd drive the stake through my heart
and put an end to the madness
that torments the immortal soul.

Night after night I rise
from my hellish confinement,
only to see my prey
and drain the flow of life from their veins.

The insatiable craving turns me into a monster—
a being I despise but cannot control.

I am cursed. I'm not human,
for I exist only as a trepid of fear
in the minds of blameless souls.
At least they have their God to protect them.
I have not—only a cold, dark coffin of wood
and dowels embedded with dirt
from a land that has come to be almost non-existent.

I dream of growing old,
of laying my head to rest at nightfall
and waking to the sun peeking up from the horizon,
falling warm upon my face.

I long to hear birds sing harmoniously,
to witness drops of dew fall delicately
against deep green leaves and velvet soft grass—
dew that sparkles greater than the finest of diamonds.
I long for the melodious sounds
of children singing and frolicking,
celebrating the newness of the day;
to wake to the warmth of another's body
wrapped snug in my own,
the smell of coffee brewing,
and the playful gestures shared
when rising from a restful night's sleep.

I have longed for hundreds of years
to once again wake and watch a rose
spread her petals, filling the Earth
with her fragrant perfume.
The smallest of things one would take for granted
are the things I miss the most.

For once I had peace,
once I had the option to die,
once I loved,
and once I cried.

Navy Man

Who can imagine the things you have seen—
wars fought in vain and wars that made history.

The seas whose waves drenched your face
saw many battles and lives fall to waste.
For all the haunts and sleepless nights,
and all the thoughts of strife,
daring to keep the fear at bay,
in dreams you ponder while in harm's way.

Comrades who embraced an unknown fate,
you were a band of brothers whose lives were at stake.
For all the anguish held inside, for all the guilt and shame,
they stood bound unto their duty, and knew it not in vain.

Shadowing haunts remain,
dreams still dark and nights the same.
Giving into tears remembering again,
your scars are evidence of your sacrifice back then.

Ships burn, bullets fly,
dodging death as it passes you by.
Hundreds of lifeless men you see lie—
there was no time for their last rites,
yet never prayer denied.
Those who escaped the reaper then
prayed his brother would find peace again.

Hand to hand, souls of men,
so much grief never forgotten.
No one knew the years you grieved,
or the evil haunts of what you have seen.
You never shared, just tucked it away,
in a secret, quiet place.
As age befell, it took you over,
and it kept you in an earthly hell.
As life ebbs and flows, as you closed your eyes,
you finally let it go.

To my hero—my Dad, the Navy man, Ellis L. Perryman
Born 11-6,1925 and Died October 27th, 2008

Happily Ever After

Bring me sunshine and roses that have not died.
Send me peace…not sacrifice.
Send me hope not walls of lies.
Help me not to think of things, that
cause me wicked dreams of tanks and death
that echo through, the enemy regimes.

A promise made to live in peace,
turned out a fantasy,
one man's quest turned inside out
destroyed the child's dream.

Before my eyes my world is crushed,
burning in cinder hell;
the fortress falls to crumbles
and destroys the secrets it could tell.

Ashes turn to dirt, metal to tetrad dust,
I've watched my world fall victim
to a man of little trust.

My minutes may be numbered now
and my moment is at hand,
my life does pass before me,
soon my soul will leave this land.

Sequestered in a corner,
I shut my tear-scorched eyes,
the fire which now consumes me,
will be my final demise.
A final fleeting thought,
comes trailing through my mind,
a child tucked in his momma's arms
brings me peace and love divine.

Dedicated to the children who died in Waco, under the influence of David Koresh, the Branch Davidian Ranch, 1993.

The Wedding

I awoke this very morn, to surroundings I've never seen before.
I was dressed in satin and flowing lace,
There were whispers of a wedding soon to take place.
Hand maidens knocking upon my door,
to assist in last minor chores.
This hand sewn gown in which I wear,
fits within the surroundings of yesteryear.

I, buried deep in my thoughts
of how I arrived in this spot,
was startled when a tear on my shoulder fell,
I turned to see through my veil,
a woman so beautiful to my sight,
it took me no time to realize
that from a picture of long ago,
great grandmother; could this be so?
Indeed those were her eyes, am I insane?

Then, she was gone as quickly as she came.
An incident passing in time,
or a well planned dream produced by my mind?
The colors exquisite, vibrant, bright,
from a distance I hear the music play,
I believe I'm expected to take the stage.

I approach this carpet of red,
the audience stands with respect.
All eyes on me I stare in misbelief;
slowly I walk, confused by my thoughts,
How did I get here?
Who is this man who awaits to take my hand?
A stranger to myself, I don't know who I am.

The minister smiles and begins to speak,
but his face, my lord, no mouth, no teeth.
Out of the corner of my left eye,
sits a coffin opened and I wonder why.
There is a fog inside this chapel, this church,
and the eeriness is growing worse.

All good senses tell me to leave,
but I'm stuck and unable to move my feet.
The groom takes hold of my hand,
and places on my finger a wedding band.
The band is green,
it is square it seems.

He plants a kiss on my right cheek,
at last I look into his eyes black and empty…
I begin to cry.
I looked back for a moment and through my tears,
a transparent figure of a thousand years,
out from the coffin arose, heading toward me
holding one black rose.

I screeched and ran for the door
but it reached from the ceiling to the floor.
I moved just in time,
as this figure approached me from behind,
then flew through the door with a frightening roar.
My heart was pounding, my head in my hand,
when this groom appeared
and spoke in a language I didn't understand,
we left out the back, I was grateful for that,
then the groom signaled to stay where I'm at.
I thought to myself, it's my chance to run,
so I fled to the woods through the sticks and stones.
I stumbled and fell, and rolled for a mile,
everything turned back for awhile.

No believe it or not, I awoke in my bed,
with an ache pruning inside my head.
There on my finger was a green square ring
and the coldest of chilled swept through me.
Something here, just wasn't right,
the sun was shining but it was still night,
and even stranger through my very own eyes,
everything around me was in black and white.
A dream, a nightmare or a dimension I crossed,
to the akashic records of recorded lifetimes I lived and lost.

The Inevitable Calling

Death is an inevitable calling
that haunts you more with age;
it becomes a reality
that you will not escape.

Forty-eight summers have passed my way—
how many more shall I make?

As we wind down and accept that fate,
we relive our life and our mistakes.

A significant price we may have to pay,
as we view our whole life
in one second of a day.

Unless, of course, it's all a joke—
and we discover it's all been a hoax.

Silence

Silence is strength;
the less murmured,
the more knowledge gained.

The more I listen,
the more I refrain.

I'm separated from here to there,
from the sounds from which I hear.

The sound of silence is bliss indeed,
but to listen is like music
that bounces off the eaves.

Silence points to nowhere,
but everywhere is loud,
because the sound of knowledge
is just waiting to come out.

I listen for the truth
to set myself apart,
but find that the process
is but a dying art.

Stardust

Further than I can reach,
lying in deep abyss,
is the pearl of my heart
and all its secrets hid.

In the darkest waters rumbling
far from human eyes,
there dwells another world,
existing but not within our sight.

Earth is but a piece of dust
that sits among the stars;
the universe is vast
and sets us all apart.

Another place, another time,
another way of life,
is far above our reach
yet so nearby.

Their bones and remnants—
a part of human stardust—
existing all together
makes them part of us.

Enigma

I am lost in the enigma
where ghosts and bare bones feast,
in a graveyard of fear that begs
through tangled vines of broken promises.

I fall victim each time I pass their way;
I hold on to faith with every fiber—
no win,
no lose,
no game,
no gain.

Separation coddles me in its mystic arms,
where I am pierced by the haunting of my worth.

Play to me a sonnet of lost laments
and sagas without meaning or torment—
then shall I listen upon deaf ears,
only to hear repeated moans
tapping at my universe,
leaving scourged remains that lie dormant
in dark puddles steeping in a fist full of rage.

Jilted

Wind creeps by soft and cold,
as day turns to night and dreams unfold.

Love shines on every fallen star,
a halo of hush in the sky so far…

It speaks again through melody and song,
to the lady in waiting for her prince to come.

Sweet turns to bitter
like the thorn of a rose,
from illusions of grandeur
to a detoured road,
She's left to wonder
why she was wronged,
why the lyrics changed
in the midst of her song.

Only a memory
of what might have been
closed the chapter to a story
with no end.

The Infinite Maze of "Me"

My thoughts weave in and out,
scurrying about,
from trains to window frames,
I see life passing through its infinite maze.

And what of my thoughts?
They run deep as an ocean,
yet never get lost.

As far as my universe can reach,
there is still so much to learn and teach.
I wonder who is me—this oh so little being.
I've never been labeled as conventional,
for my actions are sometimes less sensible.

Eclectic decisions, in my opinion;
what's clear to others is never my vision.

In my mind, at any time, I can ponder myself away,
to distant lands I've never been,
or places in which I've never lived.

So who is worthy to judge me—
my sisters or my brother?
I challenge any being to say
my thoughts are meaningless utter.

The world has never made sense to me—
look at it now, in a state of atrophy;
worry for yourself, but worry not for me.

Flying High

I'm flying high—so very high.
I'm in my plane, it's my disguise.
I'm flying high—so very high,
but this freedom still can't ease my mind.
I'm flying high—so very high,
desperately seeking my "down time."

The windows to the world I see,
interrupt my patterns of old beliefs.
Through the misty marbled cotton zone—
I've lost what used to be my own.

I'm flying high—so very high,
I see the world pass me by.
As rainbows run through the depths of my bones,
it's but another reminder—I am alone.

Watching the rain beneath my wings,
I see a lifetime in my dreams.
The barren asphalt is my sea,
and the darkened clouds now cover me.
The wind, it screams as my fear escapes,
my eyes wide shut to my mistakes.

Pieces of my years regress
and swallow up my happiness.

I'm flying so much higher now,
my dreams are turning inside out.
I'm so high I'm floating down—
it seems my time has come around.

Blinded by the light of the Son,
my mission here is almost done.
I'm heading down, so high above,
to the banks of heaven
and the face of God.

For John Denver, a truly great Singer Songwriter who died while flying his plane.

Mother Earth's Lament (Greenhouse Gods)

Mother Earth is in pain,
dying from the poison
that runs through her veins.

The autocrats who sit upon their thrones,
lie waiting to see who'll throw the biggest stone.
For Queen Oil, who rules the land,
her subjects create the endless demands.
Those who have shown a better way
find themselves in an early grave.

From the house of white bores a greedy hand,
sleazy politics that sacrificed our forefathers' plan.
We have digressed in two hundred years—
patrons of war and widows' tears,
created by the old leaders who monger us to fear,
their rule of law and corruption of their peers.

Oh leader, you have let us down,
lied and cheated with your regime of clowns.
You have no concern for my beautiful Earth;
you have raped her and left her with tainted dirt.

Once a beautiful child, alas,
you have fed her a diet of poison gas.
The saddest realization remains—
you couldn't care less you left it this way.

Rest assured, her vengeance is coming,
brewing like thunder before lightning strikes.
she'll leave you a ray of light.

What then will your oil be worth?
Forgotten like the dinosaurs beneath the earth.

Crossing Over

The sun is warming to my face,
the air smells clean as rain.

For one insidious moment,
the world has sealed my fate.

The best of a last performance,
I take my final bow,
for the curtain has descended,
and I bid my last farewell.

Reaper's watch draws nigh,
death's kiss weighs on my mind.
Falling in the sleepy light,
where lies a billowed sky,
it reaches out to touch me—
so close within my sight.

Then tossed across the sphere,
through tunnels black and light,
as voided stars in space
fall from the realm of human sight.

Dimensions drop in decibel,
till sound can't be revealed.
The phantom no longer reconciles,
as the pale hour kicks his heels.

Then in darkness fades a falling mist,
and loved ones drawing nigh—
a faint smile to the lips,
and with it, the breath of life.
In an instant, all transcends
unto the other side.

It's time for crossing over,
for the ghost has found its rest.
The soul can finally fade to sleep,
and yield its final harvest.

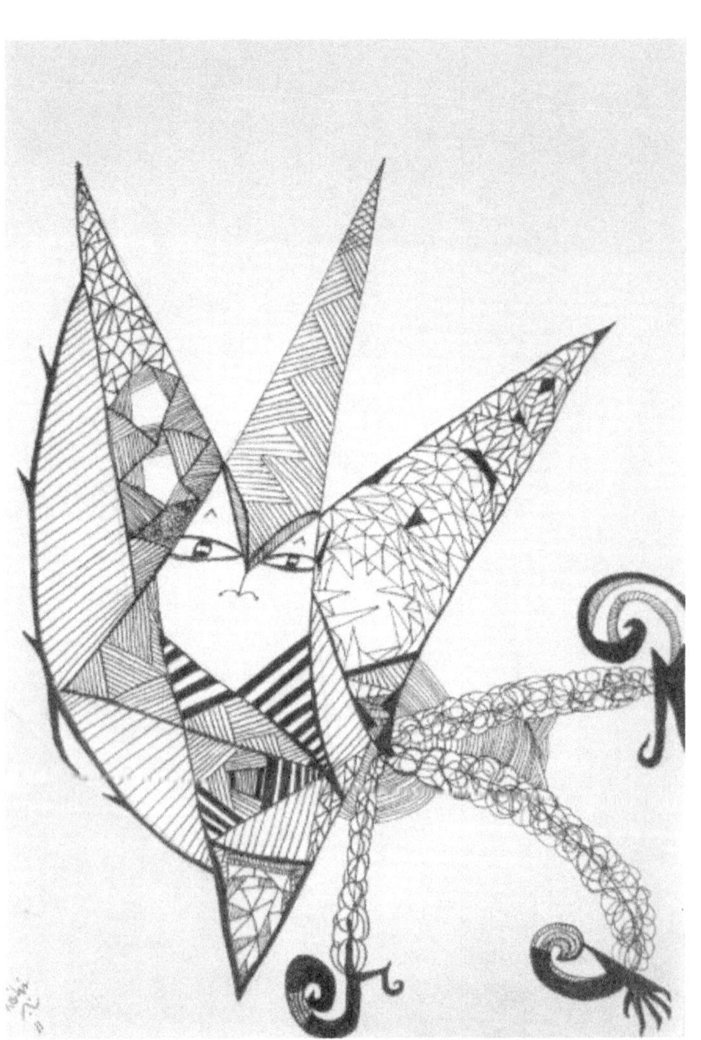

"Somewhere in Time" is a remembrance

for when I'm gone,

a piece of my soul, through it, lives on...

Kristin Elyce Perryman Hiett

Index of Poems

(In alphabetical order)

Made in the USA
Coppell, TX
09 February 2026

71478391R00114